THE RIDICULOUSLY SIMPLE GUIDE TO PIXEL 3 AND 3 XL

A PRACTICAL GUIDE TO GETTING STARTED WITH THE NEXT GENERATION OF PIXEL AND ANDROID PIE OS (VERSION 9)

D1565523

PHIL SHARP

Ridiculously Simple Press
ANAHEIM, CALIFORNIA

Table of Contents

INTRODUCTION

Google and Apple have always taken a different approach to developing their Operating System (OS). Apple's iOS is often seen as a wall gardened; it's an OS built for one thing and one thing only: the iPhone.

Unlike Apple, Google built an OS that anyone could use; in fact, Google didn't even have a phone when it released the Android OS in 2007. Its flagship phone was called the HTC Dream, and it was built, as the name suggests, by HTC.

Google was never a hardware company, but a few years back, they decided it was time to start being one. They had created an OS that was arguably superior to the iPhone, and it was time they had an official phone to go with it.

The Pixel phone was first introduced in 2016. It wasn't a terrible phone, but it simply did not stand up against the big guns of the Android OS world-- like the Galaxy and Note. Google learned a lot and the next year released a far better phone: the Pixel 2.

In 2018, Google released its best phone yet: Google Pixel 3. Photographers and critics alike praised the camera, which many consider the best mobile camera on the market. Google was finally ready for its close up.

Whether you are switching from an iPhone or another Android device, this book is for you. It will break down everything you need to know about the device and keep it ridiculously simple!

Ready to learn more? Let's get started!

[1]
START HERE

This chapter will cover:
- Setup
- Main user interface elements

SETUP

The setup is pretty intuitive, but there are still screens that might confuse you a little. If you are a self-starter and like just try things, then skip to the next section on the main UI elements of Android. If you want a more thorough walk-through, then read away!

Google knows you want to get started using your phone, so they've made the process pretty quick; most people will send about 5 or 10 minutes.

The first thing you'll see is the "Hi there" screen; you could technically make an emergency call on this screen, but I don't recommend it unless it's really an emergency--this isn't a "hey, mom, I'll be late" emergency...this is a direct to emergency responders "I've fallen and can't get up" sort of call. When you are ready to get started, tap the blue "Start" button.

You have two options on the next screen: connect to wi-fi so you can start a "SIM-free" setup or insert your SIM card.

.ıl

Connect to mobile network

If you have a SIM card, insert it now

Start SIM-free setup instead
For Project Fi and other carriers

Skip

<

If you add a SIM card you can skip all of the next steps. If you are doing SIM-Free, then tap "Start SIM-free setup instead." The next screen explains SIM-free; SIM-free is exactly what it sounds like, but it's not supported by all carriers. If your carrier supports it, then I'd recommend doing it, as everything will be stored online vs. on a card that can be easily scratched and damaged. Tap the blue "Next" to begin.

SIM-free setup

If your mobile network uses SIM-free setup, you'll get calls, texts, and data by downloading an eSIM instead of inserting a SIM card.

Next

The next screen prompts you to select your wi-fi network. This is followed by an update screen. It should take about a minute to get the latest update. When it's done, you'll see the "Copy apps & data" screen.

Copy apps & data

Transfer your apps, photos, contacts, Google Account, and more. You can choose which content to copy.

Don't copy   Next

‹

Copy apps and data is pretty resourceful. It will let you copy everything from your old phone so there's not as much to do on your new one--it works with both iPhone (through a special adaptor) and Android. It's not perfect--especially with the iPhone--but it will save you time. If you are coming from a previous generation Android phone, you can also do this without a cord by using your login. If you want to skip it and start from scratch, then select "Don't copy" in the lower left corner.

Find your old phone's cable
Use a cable that fits your old phone. This is usually the cable used for charging.

Use your old phone
You need your old Android or iPhone® device. Turn it on, and keep it unlocked.

No cable?   Next   Can't use old phone?   Next

Next, sign in to your Google Account (the one you use the check email usually--unless you don't use Gmail). If you don't have a Google Account, then click the option to create it.

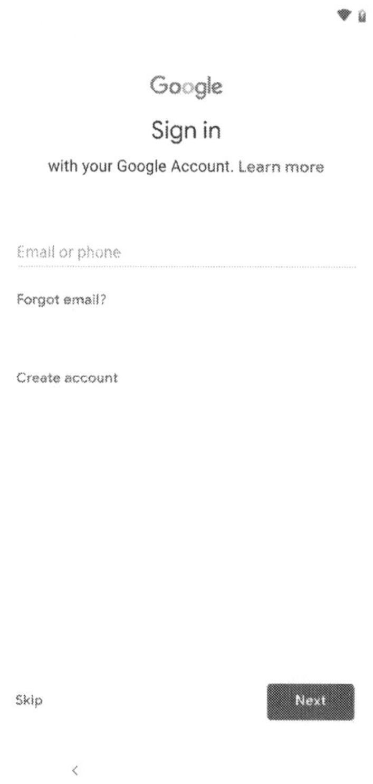

Google

Sign in

with your Google Account. Learn more

Email or phone

Forgot email?

Create account

Skip   Next

<

Once you hit next and signin, you'll get a bunch of legal stuff. It's basically saying Google's not responsible for anything. Agree to it or you just bought yourself a very expensive brick.

Google Services is the next screen. This is giving the phone permission to use features on the phone (like the fingerprint scanner, location services to see where you are at, send Google and developers crash reports, and backup your phone to the Google Drive). I recommend selecting all of them. If you are worried about privacy, I'll show you some adjustments you can make later. I should also note: if you turn them off here, you can turn them back on later.

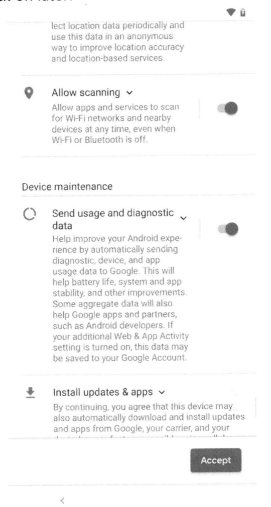

Next is yet another reminder that you can't blame Google for anything. They really want you to understand this. That way if the phone explodes in your hand, it's obviously your fault!

G

Additional legal terms

By clicking "I accept," you agree to the Google Terms of Service available at **google.com/policies/terms** and the Pixel Arbitration Agreement at **g.co/pixelarbitration**.

All disputes regarding your Google device will be resolved through BINDING ARBITRATION on an individual, non-class basis, as described in the Pixel Arbitration Agreement at **g.co/pixelarbitration**, unless you opt out by following the instructions in the Agreement.

Less info ∧

I accept

‹

If your carrier gave you a QR code to scan, then this is where you'll scan it. Just hover it under the camera within the box. If you don't have it, then just select "Don't have a QR code?" You'll be prompted to add a SIM instead. Note: You only see this screen if you didn't do "SIM-free" setup.

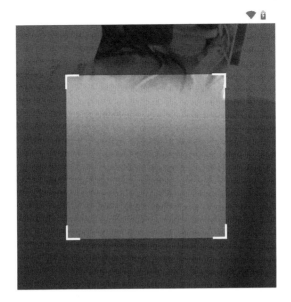

Add carrier with a QR code

If your carrier gave you a QR code, scan it now
by keeping the code centered in the box.

Enter code manually

Don't have a QR code?

‹

On the back of your phone is a fingerprint scanner. This next step will set that up for you. If you've used an iPhone, you probably used your thumb on the reader. You can do that here, but because it's on the back of the phone, your index finger is easier. The finger you use is entirely up to you.

Unlock with Pixel Imprint

Use your fingerprint to unlock your phone or approve purchases.

Note: Your fingerprint may be less secure than a strong pattern or PIN.

Skip   Next

<

Before adding a fingerprint, the next screen will ask you for a pin. If you tap "Screen lock options" you can also add a pattern. It's all a preference. My only advice is not to use a pin you use somewhere else (like a bank pin) or an easy pin (like 1234).

To use fingerprint, set PIN

For added security, set a backup screen lock

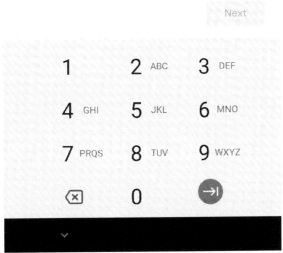

PIN must be at least 4 digits

Screen lock options

Next

1	2 ABC	3 DEF
4 GHI	5 JKL	6 MNO
7 PRQS	8 TUV	9 WXYZ
⌫	0	→|

Once you hit Next, and then reenter the pin to confirm it, you are ready to set up your finger. There's no "Next" here. Just place your finger on the reader and lift up and down slowly.

Lift, then touch again

Keep lifting your finger to add the different parts
of your fingerprint

Do it later

‹

When you are finished, you'll see a Fingerprint added screen. My advice is to tap the "Add another" in the lower left corner. You can add as many as you want, and it doesn't have to be your finger-- it could be a child or spouse. My wife uses my phone a lot, so she has her fingerprint added to the phone.

Fingerprint added

When you see this icon, use your fingerprint for
identification or to approve purchases

Add another   Next

<

Configuring Google Assistant is next. Google
Assistant is the Google equivalent of Siri. You can
tap "Leave & get reminder" but it's very quick to
do, so it's best to just get it out of the way.

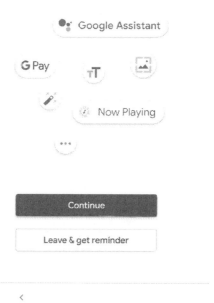

Once you agree to the terms, you are ready to go. You'll be asked a few questions (unless you have a Google Home and Google already knows your voice). The last step is to set up "Squeeze for your assistant"; this is a quick way to bring up Google Assistant--squeeze the side of your phone.

Squeeze for your Assistant

To talk to your Assistant at any time, quickly squeeze the bottom half of your phone, then release

Do it later   Next

‹

It will ask if you want a firm or soft squeeze. Once you answer and squeeze, then it's on to the "Always-on display" screen. This is asking if you want your time and notifications to always be on or if you want it on standby after a few seconds. Unless you love always see the time without pushing a button, then tap "No thanks."

Always-on display

Time, notification icons, and other info will
appear on your lock screen

No thanks   Turn on

You are just about done! The "Anything else?"
screen is your last chance to add in settings before
finishing the set up--and remember: you can
change all this later. So if you don't want to do it
now, you always can do it later. The one thing I will
point out is "Add another email account"; if you
are using this phone at work, then it's a good idea
to add in your work email here.

Anything else?

Set up a few more things now, or find them later
in Settings

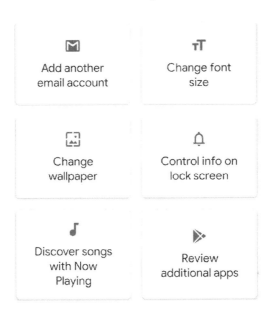

No thanks

‹

The last screen is asking if you'd like to get tip emails from Google about how to use your phone. When you are first getting started, these emails are helpful. They don't come very often.

One last tip

For support, tips and tricks, and more, go to
Settings > Tips & support

Get Pixel tips, updates on Google
products, and share feedback.
Unsubscribe any time.

All set

After a few seconds, you'll finally get to the
home screen. You are ready to use your phone!

FINDING YOUR WAY AROUND

People come to the Pixel from all sorts of different places: iPhone, other Android phone, flip phone, two styrofoam cups tied together with string. This next section is a crash course in the interface. If you've used Android before, then it might seem a little simple, so skip ahead if you already know all of this.

If any of this seems a little rushed, there's good reason: it is! We'll cover these points in more detail later. This is just a quick starter / reference.

On the bottom of your screen is the shortcut bar--you'll be spending a lot of time here; you can add whatever you want to this area, but these are the apps Google thinks you'll use most--and, with the exception of the Play Store, they are probably right.

So what are these? Real quick, these are as follows:

- **Phone**: Do you want to take a wild guess what the phone button does? If you said brings you an ice cream, then maybe you aren't cut out for a phone. But if you said something along the lines of "It launches an app to call people" then you'll have no problem at all with your new device. Suprises, surprise: this pricey gadget that plays games, takes pictures, and keeps you up-to-date on political ramblings on social media does one more interesting thing: it calls people!

- **Message**: Message might be a little more open-ended than "Phone"; that could mean email message, text messages, messages you keep getting on your bathroom mirror to put the toilet seat down. In this case, it means "text messages" (but really--put that toilet seat down...you aren't doing anyone any favors). This is the app you'll use whenever you want to text cute pictures of cats.
- **Play Store**: Anything with the word "Play" in the title must be fun, right?! This app is what you'll use to download all those fun apps you always hear about.
- **Chrome**: Whenever you want to surf the Internet, you'll use Chrome. There are actually several apps that do the same thing--like Firefox and Opera--but I recommend Chrome until you are comfortable with your phone. Personally, I think it's the best app for searching the Internet, but you'll soon learn that most things on the phone are about preference, and you may find another Internet browser that suits your needs more.
- **Camera**: This apps opens pictures of vintage cameras...just kidding! It's how you take pictures on your phone. You use this same app for videos as well.

Next, to the shortcut bar, the area you'll use the most is the notification bar. This is where you'll get, you guessed it, notifications! What's a notification? That's any kind of notice you have elected to receive. A few examples: text message alerts, email alerts, amber alerts, and apps that have updates.

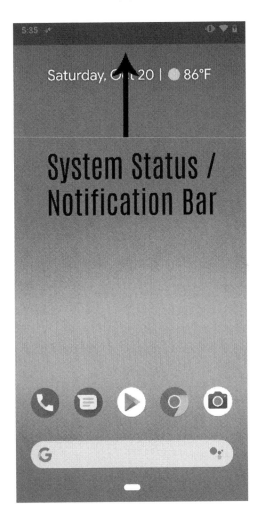

When you drag your finger down from the notification bar, you'll get a list of several settings that you can adjust. Press and hold any of these options and you'll open an app with even more options.

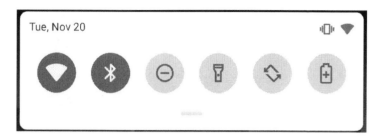

From right to left these are the options you can change or use:

- Wifi
- Bluetooth
- Do not disturb
- Flashlight
- Lock the device from auto-rotating
- Turn on / off battery saving

If you continue dragging down, this thin menu expands and there are a few more options--four to be exact.

The first is at the top of the screen--it's the slider, and it makes your device brighter or dimmer depending on which way you drag it.

On the bottom row there are three other options that weren't in the smaller menu:

- **Data**--tapping this turns your data on and off, which is handy if you are running low on data and don't want to be charged extra for it.

- **Airplane mode** - this turns off Bluetooth, data, and wifi and makes your device ready to use on an airplane.

- **Night light** - This is a special mode that dims your screen and makes the screen appropriate for reading in dark settings.

You may have noticed something that seems important missing from your phone: a home bottom. On older phones, this was a critical button that gets you to the home screen whenever you push it.

How on Earth do you get Home without a Home button?! Enter the digital Home button! That's the tiny line on the bottom of your screen.

Push that button and you get home. Additionally, you can swipe up from that button and see the most recent apps.

If you've used any Apple device, then you might know a thing or two about Siri. She's the assistant that "sometimes" works; Google has its own version of Siri and it's called Google Assistant. The names not quite as creative as Siri, but many say it works better. I'll let you be the judge of that.

To get to the Google Assistant from anywhere, just say "Ok, Google." If you are on the home screen, then there's also a Google Assistant widget. This little bar does more than make appointments and get your information--it's also a global search. What does mean? It means you can type in anything you want to know and it will search both the Internet and your phone. If it's a contact in your phone, then it will get you that. But if it's the opening hours for the Museum of Strange then it will search the Internet--it will also give you a map of the location and the phone number.

[2]

THE RIDICULOUSLY SIMPLE OVERVIEW OF ALL THE THINGS YOU SHOULD KNOW

This chapter will cover:
- Customizing screens
- Split screens
- Gestures

MAKING PRETTY SCREENS

If you've used an iPhone or iPad, then you may notice the screen looks a little...bare. There's literally nothing on it. Maybe you like that. If so, then good for you! Skip ahead. If you want to decorate that screen with shortcuts and widgets, then read on.

ADDING SHORTCUTS

Any app you want on this screen, just find it, and then press and hold; when a menu comes up, drag it upward until the screen appears and move it to where you want it to go. You can also drag it to new screens.

To remove an app from a screen, tap and hold, then drag it upward to the Remove text that appears when you move it up. When it's there, let go.

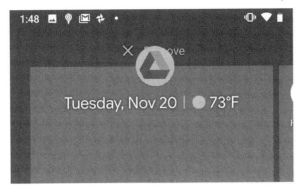

WIDGETS

Shortcuts are nice, but widgets are better. Widgets are sort of like mini-programs that run on your screen. A common widget people put on their screen is the weather forecast. Throughout the day the widget will update automatically with up to the date info.

To add a widget, go to the screen you want to add it to and tap and hold until the menu comes up.

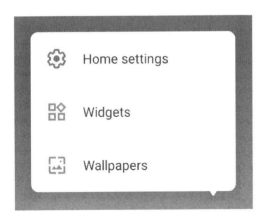

Select Widgets. This opens up a widget library--
it's like a mini app store.

When you find one you want to add, tap and
hold it, then drag it to the screen you want to add
it to.

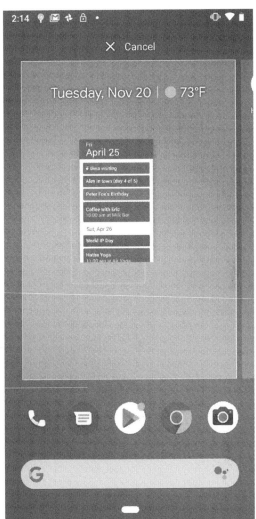

Widgets come in all sorts of shapes and sizes, but most of them can be resized. To resize it, tap and hold it. If you see little circles, then you can tap those and drag it in or out to make it bigger or smaller.

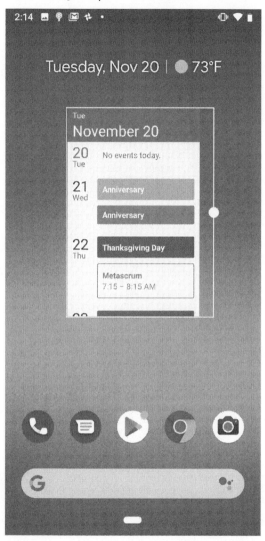

You remove widgets the same way you remove shortcuts. Tap and hold and then drag it upward to the remove.

WALLPAPER

Adding wallpaper to your screen is done in a similar way. Tap and hold your finger on the home screen, when the menu comes up, select Wallpaper instead of Widgets. Some of the options even move--so the wallpaper always has something moving across your screen--it's like a slow moving movie.

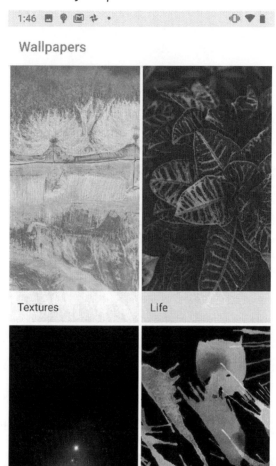

When you have a wallpaper open that you want to add, just hit the Set Wallpaper in the upper right corner.

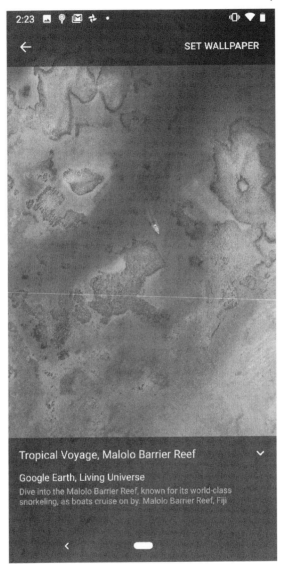

A WORD, OR TWO, ABOUT MENUS

It's pretty intuitive that if you tap on an icon, it opens the app. What's not so obvious is if you tap and hold there are other options. Every app is different. Usually, they're shortcuts--tapping and holding over the Phone icon, for example, brings up your favorites; doing the same thing over the camera brings up a selfie mode shortcut. Tap and hold over your favorite apps to see what shortcuts are available.

SPIT SCREENS

The Pixel phone comes in two different sizes; the bigger screen obviously gives you a lot more space, which makes split screen apps a pretty handy feature. It works on the smaller Pixel as well, though it doesn't feel as effective on the smaller screen.

To use this feature, swipe up to bring up multitasking; next, tap the icon above the window you want to turn into split screen (note: this feature is not supported on all apps); if split screen is available, you'll see a menu that has an option for split screen.

Once you tap split screen, it will let you swipe left and right to find the app you want to split the screen with. Tap the one you want.

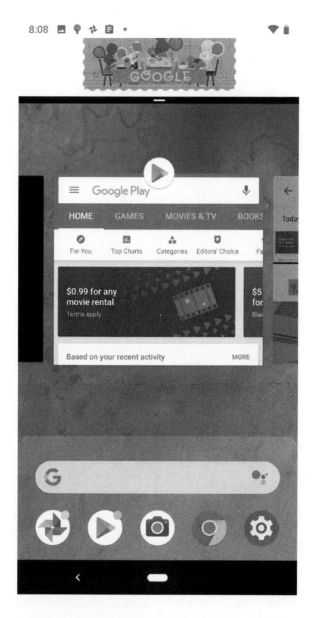

Your screen is now split in two.

That thin black bar in the middle is adjustable; you can move it up or down so one of the apps has more screen real estate.

To exit this mode, drag the black bar either all the way to the top or all the way to the bottom until one of the apps completely goes away.

GESTURES

ACTIVE EDGE

Squeeze your phone on the bottom sides to open up your Google Assistant. If your phone is ringing, you can also squeeze to silence the notification.

JUMP TO CAMERA

Press the power button twice to quickly jump to the camera.

FLIP CAMERA

Switch in and out of selfie mode while you are in the camera by double-twisting the phone.

DOUBLE-TAP

If your phone is in standby, double tap the screen and the time and notifications will appear.

[3]

THE BASICS…AND KEEP IT RIDICULOUSLY SIMPLE

This chapter will cover:
- Making calls
- Sending messages
- Finding and downloading apps
- Driving directions

Now that you have your phone setup and know your way around the device at it's most basic level, let's go over the apps you'll be using the most that are currently on your shortcut or favorite bar:
- Phone
- Messages
- Google Play Store
- Chrome

Notice that Camera is off this list? There's a lot to cover with camera, so I'll go over it in a separate chapter.

Before we get into it, there's something you need to know: how to open apps not on your favorite bar. It's easy. Remember that Home button on the bottom that you can press to get back to your home screen? Go to that, but don't press it once: hold it, and keep holding it as you swipe up all the way to the top of your screen. Notice that menu that's appearing? That's where all the additional apps are.

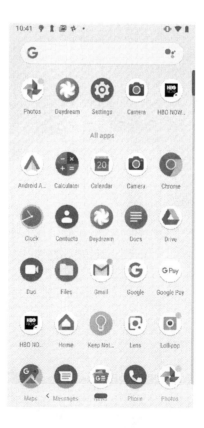

MAKING CALLS

So...who you going to call? Ghostbusters?!

You would be the most awesome person in the world if Ghostbusters was in your phone contacts! But before you can find that number in your contacts, it would probably help to know how to add a contact, find a contact, edit a contact, and put contacts into groups, right? So before we get to making calls, let's do baby steps and cover Contacts.

CONTACTS

So let's open up the Contacts app to get started. See it? Not on your favorite bar, right? So where is it?! That's why I showed you earlier how to get to additional apps. Swipe up from the bottom of your screen and keep swiping until the menu appears in its entirety.

It's in alphabetical order, so the Contacts app is in the C's. It looks like this:

Contacts

Chances are if you've added your email account, you'll already have a lot of contacts listed. Like hundreds!

You can either scroll slowly, or head to the right-hand side of the app and scroll--this lets you quickly scroll by letters. Just slide your finger until you see the letter of the contact you want and then stop.

I'm getting ahead of myself, however! Before you can scroll, it would be nice to know how to add a contact so there are people to scroll to. To add a contact, tap on that blue plus sign.

Adding a person looks more like applying for a job than adding a contact. There are rows and rows of fields!

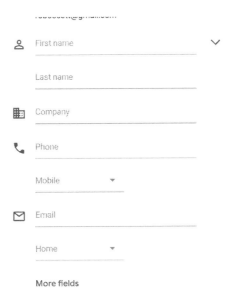

Just in case you weren't overwhelmed by all the fields, you can tap more fields and get even more!

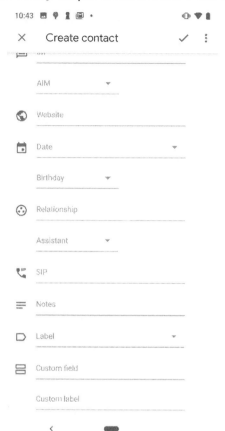

Is that not enough? Google has you covered because you can add a custom field!

Here's the most important thing you need to know: fields are optional! You can add a name and email and that's it. You don't even have to add their phone number. If you want to call them, then that would certainly help though.

If you have a hard time remembering who people are, then you can also take a picture or add a picture you already have. Comes in handy if you have eight kids and you can't remember if Joey is the one with blonde hair or red hair.

Once you are done, tap the checkbox. That saves it. If you decide you don't want to add a contact afterall, the tap the X. That closes it without saving.

EDITING A CONTACT

If you add an email and then later decide you should add a phone number, or if you want to edit anything else, then just find the name in your contacts and tap it once. This brings up all the info you've already added.

Go to the lower corner and tap on the pencil button. This makes the contact editable. Go to

your desired filled and update. When you are finished tap the checkbox in the upper right corner.

SHARING A CONTACT

If you have your phone long enough, someone
will ask you for so and so's phone number. The old
fashion way was to write it down. But you have a
smartphone, so you aren't old fashion!

The new way to share a number is to find the
person in your contacts, tap their name, then tap
those three dots in the upper right corner of your
screen. This brings up a menu.

Delete

Share

Add to Home screen

Set ringtone

Route to voicemail

Help & feedback

There are a few options here, but the one you want is "Share"; from here you have a few options, but the easiest is to text or email the contact to your friend. This sends them a contact card. So if you have other information with that contact (such as email) then that will be sent over as well.

DELETE CONTACT

There are a few more options on that menu I just showed. If you decide a person is dead to you and you never want to contact them again, then you can return to that menu and tap Delete. This erases them from your phone, but not your life.

GET ORGANIZED

Once you start getting lots of contacts, then it's going to make finding someone more time-consuming. Labels helps. You can add a label for "Family" for instance, and then stick all of your family members there.

When you open your contacts and tap those three lines in the upper left corner, you'll see a menu. This is where you'll see your labels. So with labels, you can jump right into that list and find the contact you need.

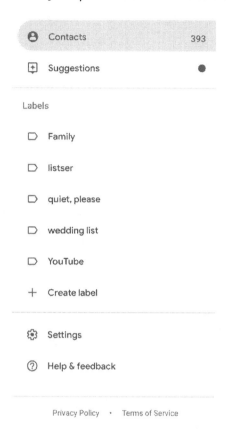

You can also send the entire group inside the label an email or text message. So for instance, if your child is turning 2 and you want to remind everyone in your "Family" contact not to come, then just tap on that label, and then tap on the three dots in the upper right corner. This brings up a menu of options.

Send email

Send message

Remove contacts

Rename label

Delete label

From here, just tap send email or send message.

But what if you don't have labels? Or if you want to add people to a label? Easy. Remember that long application you used to add a contact? One of the fields was called "Labels". You have to tap more to see it. It's all the way at the bottom. One of the last fields, in fact.

If you've never added a label or want to add a new one, then just start typing. If you have another one that you'd like to use, then just tap the arrow and select it.

When you are done, don't forget to tap Save.

DELETE LABEL

If you decide you no longer want to have a label, then just go to the menu I showed you above--side menu, then the three dots. From here, tap the Delete Label.

If there's just one person you want to boot from the label, then tap them and go to the label and delete it.

MAKING CALLS

That concludes are sidetrack into the Contacts app. We can now return to getting back to making phone calls to the Ghostbusters.

You can make a call by opening the Contacts app, then selecting the contact, and then tapping on their phone number. Alternatively, you can tap on the Phone button from your Home screen or favorite bar.

There are a few options when you open this app. Let's talk about each one.

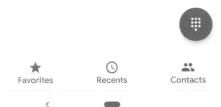

Starting from the far left is the Favorites tab. If you tap this, then you'll see your favorite contacts. If you haven't added any, then this will be empty. If you want to make someone your favorite, then tap them in your Contacts, and tap the star on the top by their name. Once you do that, they'll automatically start showing up here.

In the middle is the "Recent" tab. If you've made any calls, they'll show here.

The last option is Contacts, which opens a version of the Contacts app that's within the Phone app.

Also on the right is the dial button.

If you want to dial someone the old fashion way by tapping in numbers, then tap this.

When you are done with the call, hit the End button on your phone.

ANSWER AND DECLINE CALLS

What do you do when someone calls you? Probably ignore it because it's a telemarketer!

It's easy to accept a call, however. When the phone rings, the number will appear and if the person is in your contacts, then the name will appear as well. To answer, just swipe the answer. To decline just drag the decline.

Play Angry Birds While Talking to Angry Mom

What if you're on a call with your mom and she's just complaining about something, but you don't want to be rude and hang up? Easy. You multitask! This means you could play Angry Birds while talking!

To multitask, just swipe up from the bottom of your phone, and open the app you want to work in while you are talking. The call will show in the notification area. Tap it to return to the call.

MESSAGES

Now that you know how Contacts and Phone works, messaging will be like second nature. They share many of the same properties.

Let's open up the Messages app (it's on your Favorites bar).

CREATE / SEND A MESSAGE

When you have selected the contact(s) to send a message to, tap Compose. You can also manually type in the number in the text field.

You can add more than one contact--this is known as a group text.

Use the text field to type out your message. If you want add anything fancy to your message (like photos or gifs) then tap the plus sign. This brings up a menu with more options.

When you are ready to send your message, tap the arrow with the SMS under it.

VIEW MESSAGE

When you get a message, your phone will vibrate, chip, or do nothing--it all depends on how you set up your phone. To view the message, you can either open the app, or swipe down to see your notifications--one will be the text message.

WHERE'S AN APP FOR THAT?

I mentioned earlier that you could play Angry Birds while talking to your angry mom on the phone. Sound fun? But where is Angry Birds on your phone? It's not! You have to download it.

Adding and removing apps on the Pixel is easy. Head to your favorite bar on the bottom of your home screen and tap the Google Play app.

This launches the Play Store.

From here you can browse the top apps, see editors picks, look through categories, or, if you have an app in mind, search for it. The Play Store isn't just for apps. You can use the tabs on the top to go to movies, books, and music. Any kind of downloadable content that's offered by Google can be found here.

When you see the app you want, tap on it. You can read through reviews, see screenshots, and install it on your phone. To install, simply tap the install button--if it's a paid app you'll be prompted to buy it. If there's no price, its' free (or offers in-app payments--which means the app is free, but there are premium features inside it you may have to pay for.)

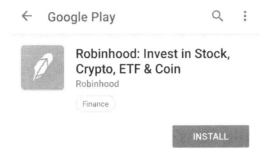

The app is now stored in the app section of your device (remember the section you get to when you swipe up from the bottom to the top?)

REMOVE APP

If you decide you no longer want an app, go to the app in the app menu and tap and hold it. This brings up a box that says "App info." Tap that.

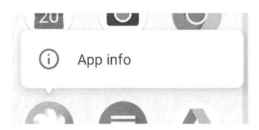

From this menu, you'll get all the information about the app; one of the options is to remove it. Tap that and you're done.

Uninstall	Force stop

Notifications
On

Permissions
No permissions granted

Storage
153 MB used in internal storage

Data usage
82.75 MB used since Oct 25

Advanced
Time spent in app, Battery, Open by default, Sto..

If you download the app from the Play store, you can always delete it. Some apps that were pre-installed on your phone cannot be deleted.

DRIVING DIRECTIONS

Back in the day, you may have had a GPS. It was a fancy plastic device that would give you directions for anywhere in North America. You can throw out that device because your phone is your new GPS.

To get directions, swipe up to open up your apps. Tap the Maps app.

Maps

It's automatically going to be set to wherever you are currently at--which is both creepy and useful.

To get started, just type where you want to go. I'm searching for Disneyland, Anaheim.

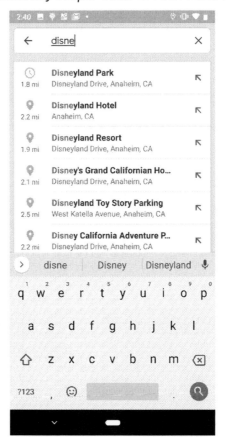

It automatically starts filling in what it thinks you are going to type and tells you the distance. When you see the one you want, tap it.

It pinpoints the location on the map and also gives you an option to call, share or get directions to the location. If you want to zoom out or in, just use two fingers and pinch in or out on the screen.

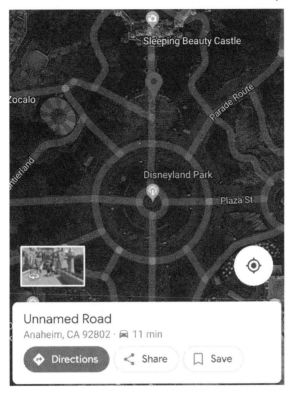

It automatically gets directions from where you are. Want it from a different location? Just tap on the "Your location" field and type where you want to go. You can also reverse the directions by tapping on the double arrows. When you are ready to go, tap "Start."

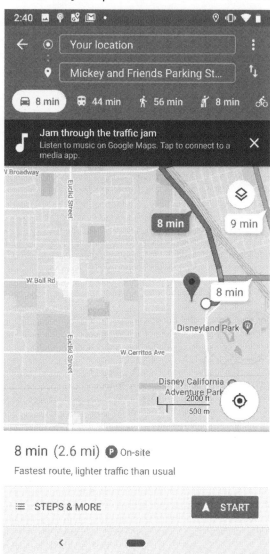

What if you don't want to drive? What if you want to walk? Or Bike? Or take a taxi? There are options for all of those and more! Tap the slider under the address bar to whatever you prefer. This updates the directions--when you walk, for example, it will show you one-way streets and also update the time it will take you.

What if you want to drive but are like me: terrified of freeways in California? There's an option to avoid highways. Tap the menu button in the upper right corner of the screen, then select what you want to avoid, and hit done. You are now rerouted to a longer route--notice how the times probably changed?

Options

☐   Avoid highways

☐   Avoid tolls

☐   Avoid ferries

CANCEL   DONE

Once you get your directions, you can swipe up to get turn-by-turn directions. You can even see what it looks like from the street. It's called Street View.

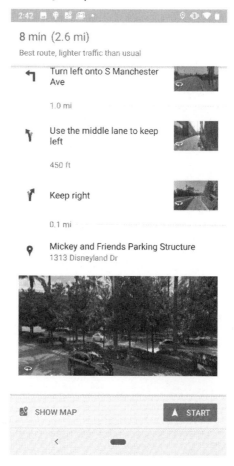

Street View isn't only for streets. Google is expanding the feature everywhere. If you hold your finger over the map, there will be an option to show Street View if it's available. Just tap the thumbnail. Here's a Street View of Disneyland:

You can wander around the entire park! If only you could ride the rides too! You can get even closer to the action by picking up the Dreamview headset. When you stick your phone in that, you can turn your head and the view turns with you.

Street View is also available in a lot of malls and other tourist attractions. Point your map to the Smithsonian in Washington, DC and get a pretty cool Street View.

[4]

LET'S GO SURFING NOW!

This chapter will cover:
- Setting up email
- Creating and send email
- Managing multiple accounts
- Browsing the Internet

When it comes to the Internet, there are two things you'll want to do:
- Send email
- Browse the Internet

ADD AN EMAIL ACCOUNT

When you set up your phone, you'll set it up to your Google Account, which is usually your email.

You may, however, want to add another email account--or remove the one you set up.

To add an email, swipe up to bring up your apps, and tap on Settings.

Next, tap on Accounts.

From here, select "Add Account"; you can also tap on the account that's been set up and tap re-move account--but remember you can have more than one accounts on your phone.

Once you add your email, you'll be asked what type of email it is. Follow the steps after you select the email type to add in your email, password, and other required fields.

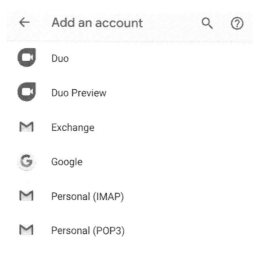

CREATE AND SEND AN EMAIL

To send an email using Gmail (Pixel's native email app), swipe up to get to your apps, tap

Gmail, and tap Compose a New Email (the little round red pencil in the lower right corner). When you're done, tap the send button.

You can also use the Google Play Store to find other email apps (such as Outlook).

MANAGE MULTIPLE EMAIL ACCOUNTS

If you have more than one Gmail account, tap the three lines at the upper left of your email screen; this brings out a slider menu. If you tap on the little arrow next to the email address, it drops down and will show other accounts. If known are listed, you can add one.

SURFING THE INTERNET

Google's native Web browser is Chrome. You can use other browsers (which can be found in the Google Play Store). This book will only cover Chrome, however.

Get started by tapping on the Chrome browser icon from your favorite bar, or by going into all progams.

If you've used Chrome on a desktop or any other device, then this chapter won't exactly be rocket science--just like the email app, many of the same properties you find on the desktop exist on the mobile version.

When you open it, you'll see it's a pretty basic browser. There are three main things that you'll want to note.

- **Address Bar** - As you would guess, this is where you put the Internet address you want to go to (google.com, for example); what you should understand, however that this is not just an address bar. This is a search bar. You can use it to search for things just as you would searching for something on Google; when you hit the enter key, it takes you to the Google search results page.

- Tab Button - Because you are limited in space, you don't actually see all your tabs like you would on a normal browser; instead you get a button that tells you how many tabs are open. If you tap it, you can either toggle between the tabs, or swipe over one of the pages to close the tab.

- **Menu Button** - The last button brings up a menu with a series of other options that I'll talk about next.

→ ☆ ⬇ ⓘ ↻

New tab

New incognito tab

Bookmarks

Recent tabs

History

Downloads

Share...

Find in page

Add to Home screen

Desktop site   ☐

Settings

Help & feedback

The menu is pretty straightforward, but there are a few things worth noting.

New incognito tab opens your computer into private browsing; that doesn't mean your IP isn't tracked. It means your history isn't record; it also means passwords and cookies aren't stored.

A little bit further down is History; if you want your history erased so there's no record on your phone of where you went, then go here, and clear your browsing history.

History   ⓘ 🔍 ✕

Your Google Account may have other forms of browsing history at myactivity.google.com.

CLEAR BROWSING DATA...

If you want to erase more than just websites (passwords, for example) then go to Settings at the very bottom of the menu. This opens up more advance settings.

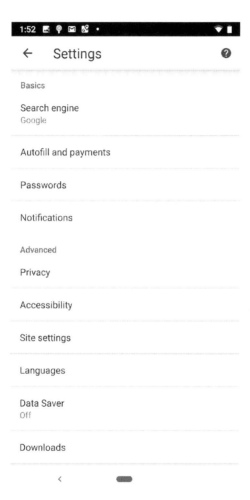

[5]

SNAP IT!

This chapter will cover:
- How to take different photos
- How to take videos
- Camera settings
- Different camera features

The camera is the bread and butter of the Pixel phone. Many people consider the Pixel to be the greatest camera ever on a phone. I'll leave that for you to decide.

One of the nice things about photos on the Pixel is it stores them online automatically, so you don't have to worry about losing them. You can see them by logging into the Google account associated with your Pixel and going here:

https://photos.google.com

You can also make edits to the photos.

Best of all: this is all free! You don't have to pay extra for more storage and it doesn't go against other things in your Google Drive. So you can up- load hours and hours of 4K video and it won't cost you a dime.

To make sure you have this feature on, go to Settings and Backup and sync; make sure you tog- gle it on.

The feature will work until January 31, 2022; by then cloud storage will be probably be pretty cheap or Google will have another solution for you. Or you could just download everything at that time to a physical hard drive and continue to pay noth- ing.

Are you ready to get your Ansel Adams on? Let's get started by opening the camera app. You can do this several ways:

- The most obvious is to tap the Camera on your favorite bar or by swiping up and opening it from all apps. It looks like a camera--go figure!

Camera

- Double press the power button.

Once you are in the app, don't forget, you can twist the phone to toggle between selfie mode.

When you open the app, it always starts in the basic camera mode. No matter what mode you are in, you will see two navigation UI elements that are always the same:

The top menu bar, which is where you control things like tempature, add a timer, turn off flash.

And the bottom menu bar, which is where you'll see the selfie button, the shutter, and the last photo taken.

These UI elements change depending on what mode you are in. Some will have extra options, and others will have fewer options. But the size and layout will be consistently the same--so, for example, you always know the flash option will be on top and the shutter button will always be on the bottom.

Let's look at each of the modes next.

Think of modes like different lenes. You have your basic camera lens, but then you can also have a lens for fisheye, and close up. If you look at the bottom of your camera app, you can slide left and right to get to the different modes. The first one is Panorama.

Panorama is great for landscape photos. The below photo is an example (note: this was not shot on the Pixel):

The way it works on the Pixel, is you take one photo, and then you move a little to the right and take a nother, and so on and so forth; then all of those photos are stitched together to make one giant photo. Just hit the arrow button for each button and the blue button to finish (or X button to cancel)

Next to Panorama is the portrait. Portrait mode gives your photos a sharp professional look to them. It blurs the background to really make your photos pop. I'll show an example with a photo of myself--apologies in advance for my looks!

Here I am with zero blur:

And here I am with maximum blur:

So how do you do that? First, slide to the Portrait mode. The phone will try and figure out where the focal point will be, but you'll get the best effect if you tap on the screen where the focus will be. If you tap on the face, for example, it will tell the phone you want to blur everything else. The change won't be noticeable--you can edit it after.

There's a few things you can optimize before taking the shot. First, look on that top row. It's changed a little. There's four options:

- **Retouching** - If you want to really show all the pores and features of a person, then you can turn off retouching; if you want to give faces a smoother look, then there's natural and soft retouching.

- **Timer** - Sets a timer so you can take a family photo.

- **Environment** - By default, this is set to Auto, but if you want to manually tell the phone about your environment (if you are outside and it's about to rain, for example) then you can do so here; it will change the lighting to reflect that environment.

- **Flash** - Toggles flash from on, off, and auto.

When you tap the screen, you'll see a few more options. One is in the lower right corner and looks like a magnifying glass with two arrows.

Tap that and it opens up a Zoom slider--slide in and out to move closer or further to an object.

On the left side is also the temperature gauge; you can make the photo lighter or darker before you take it.

Once you press the shutter to take the photo, you can edit the blur by doing one of two things.

Two the right of the shutter, you'll see a round shape with the photo; tap that to edit it.

Go to all apps by swiping up, and tapping on photos.

Once your photo is open, go to the row on the bottom.

This row has five options:
- Share the photo
- Edit the photo
- Keep only one photo (Google takes several shots and will show you the best one)
- Turn on lens (I'll cover this below)
- Delete the photo

The option you want is the second: edit the photo.

Tapping this brings up an option to change the saturation of the photo--you can slide to the right and see all the options.

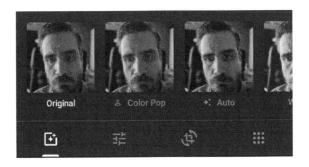

On the bottom, you'll see a little control button: tap that.

This brings another set of options; the bottom option is depth. That's what you want to change to edit the blur.

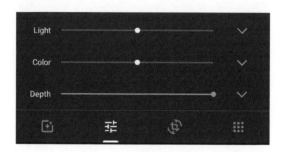

Note: depth is only available on portrait photos.

Next let's move the slider over to Camera; this is the default camera. It works the same as Portrait, but there's different options. See the A with the partial circle around it in the example below?

That turns motion on, off, or sets it to auto. Motion means when you take a photo, it takes a very short video, so you can see what happened before the shot. It's fun for kids photos and action shots, but it also takes up a lot of space. If you are short on space, it's a good idea to turn it off.

You can edit the photo the same way you would the Portrait mode, but you'll notice depth is gone. In its place, it says "Pop." It makes the focal point stand out more, but does not have the same blur effect.

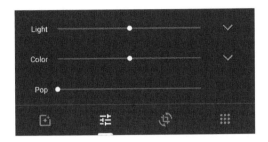

Next to the camera is the video. The video is pretty basic. If you tap the image, it will focus on it and give you the same option on the side to zoom in and out, and brighten or darken the image.

The shutter itself has changed appearances, but still is in the same place.

On top, the options are even more limited: frames per second, environment, and flash.

Frames per second brings up an option to set it to auto or 30 frames. 30 frames would be 4K and would take up more storage.

The last option you'll see on the slider says "More". Tapping this brings up several additional modes that you probably won't use quite as much. With the exception of Night Sight, these are more fun modes.

The modes are as follows:

- **Night sight** - If you are in an area with low light (i.e. a night environment) then you'll probably see an option to turn this on automatically. This mode helps you capture those kind of shots a little more accurately. You'll never get the same quality you will in areas with good light, but this mode helps you out a lot.

- The shutter in this mode changes to a moon; to exit the mode, tap the X in the upper left corner.

- **Photo Sphere** - Remember I talked about how you could walk through Disneyland in Street View? Those kind of shots are made possible, in part, because of Photo Sphere. I don't know that this is how those shots were captured, but that's the kind of photos you get with these? You could just as easily call it 360 photos.On the top of the mode, there's an option to change the spherical shape of your photo if you don't want it to be 360.

- **Photobooth** - This mode takes several photos just as an old fashion photobooth would.

- **Slow Motion** - This is a video mode that captures videos in, you guessed it, slow motion.

- **Playground** - Google is experimenting a lot in the world of augmented reality (AI); that's what this mode is all about. You an put popular Star Wars and Marvel characters into your photo or video.

- **Lens** - This mode takes a photo, but what it really does is performs an image search; what do I mean? Let's say you want to know what purse someone is holding--take a picture in this mode and it will tell you what it is. It's not always incredibly accurate, but it's still fun to play around with.

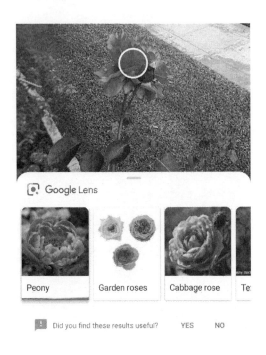

After you are done talking photos, you can open up the Photo app, and create folders and slideshows of them. To do this, tap on the photo you want to add to a folder (or tap and hold to add several), then tap the menu in the upper right corner.

Info

Slideshow

Move to folder

Copy to folder

Add to album

Use as

Print

Edit in Markup

Delete from device

[6]

GOING BEYOND

This chapter will cover:
- System settings

If you want to take total control of your Pixel, then you need to know where the system settings are and what can and can't be changed there.

First the easy: the system setting is located with the rest of your apps. Swipes up, and scroll down to "Settings."

Settings

This opens all the settings available:

- Network & Internet
- Connected devices
- Apps & notification
- Battery
- Display
- Sound
- Storage
- Security & location
- Accounts
- Accessibility
- Digital Wellbeing
- Google
- System
- Tips & support

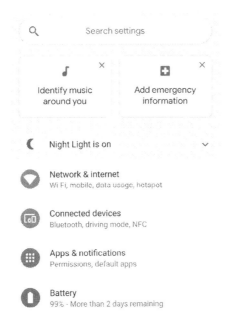

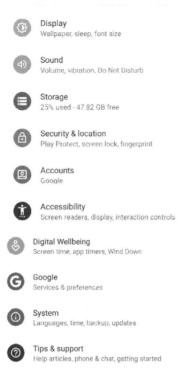

Display
Wallpaper, sleep, font size

Sound
Volume, vibration, Do Not Disturb

Storage
25% used - 47.82 GB free

Security & location
Play Protect, screen lock, fingerprint

Accounts
Google

Accessibility
Screen readers, display, interaction controls

Digital Wellbeing
Screen time, app timers, Wind Down

Google
Services & preferences

System
Languages, time, backup, updates

Tips & support
Help articles, phone & chat, getting started

I'll cover what each setting does in this chapter.

NETWORK & INTERNET

This setting, like most settings, does exactly what it sounds like: connects to the Internet. If you need to connect to a new wireless connection (or disconnect from one) you can do it here. Tapping on the current wireless lets you see other networks, and the toggle lets you switch it on and off.

Mobile network is for your carrier (Verizon, AT&T, Sprint, etc)

Data usage tells you how much data you've used; tapping on it gives you a deeper overview, so you can see exactly what apps used the data. Why is this important? For most, it probably won't be. I'll give an example of when it helped me: I work on the go a lot; I use the wireless on my phone to connect my laptop (which is called tethering); my MacBook was set to back-up to the cloud, and little did I know it was doing this while connecting to my phone...20GB later, I was able to pinpoint what happened by looking at the data.

Below this is Hotspot & tethering. This is when you use your phones data to connect other devices; you can use your phones data plan, for example, to use the Internet on your iPad. Some carriers charge extra for this--mine (AT&T) includes it in the plan. To use it, tap the setting and turn it on, then name your network and password. From your other device, you find the network you set up, and connect.

Airplane mode is next. This setting turns off all wireless activity with a switch. So if your flying and they tell you to turn everything wireless of, you can do it with a switch.

Finally "Advanced" is for doing some wireless connecting on a private network. This is not something a beginning user would need to do, and I'm not going to cover it, as the point of this book is to keep it ridiculously simple.

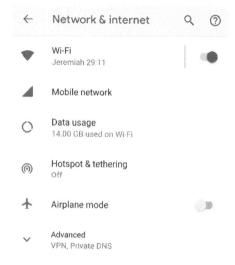

CONNECTED DEVICES

"Connected devices" is Google's way of saying Bluetooth. If you have something that connects via Bluetooth (such as a car radio or headphones) then tap "Pair new device." If you've previously paired something, then it will show below and you can simply tap it to reconnect.

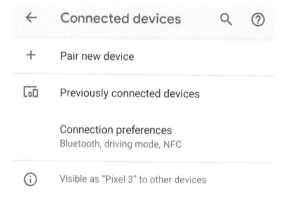

APPS & NOTIFICATION

Every app you download have different settings and permissions. A map app, for example, needs your permission to know your location. You can turn these permissions on and off here. Does it really matter? App makers can't abuse, right? Sort of. Here's an example: a few months ago, a popular ride-sharing app made headlines because it wanted to know where passengers were after they left the ride, so they could promote different restaurants and stores and make even more money. Many felt this was both greedy and an invasion of privacy; if you are of the latter stance, then you could go in here and stop sharing your location.

How? Just tap "Advance" then look at all the permissions you are giving away. Go to the permission you are concerned with and toggle the app from on to off.

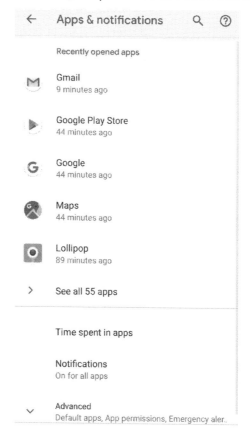

BATTERY

The battery setting is more about analytics then settings you can change. There are some settings here you can edit--you can put your phone in battery saving mode, for example. This setting is more useful if your battery is draining too quickly; it helps you troubleshoot what's going on so you can get more life from your phone.

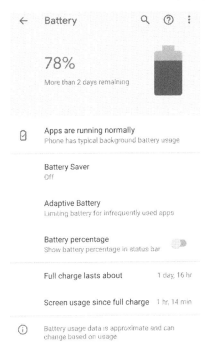

DISPLAY

As with most the settings, almost all the main features of the Display setting can be changed outside of the app. If you tap "Advanced," however, you'll see some settings, not in other places. These include changing colors and font sizes.

← Display   🔍 ⑦

Brightness level
64%

Night Light
On / Will never turn off automatically

Adaptive brightness
Optimize brightness level for available light

Wallpaper

⌄ **Advanced**
Sleep, Auto-rotate screen, Colors, Font size, Dis..

SOUND

There's a volume button on the side of your phone, so why would you need to open up a setting for it?! This setting lets you get more specific about your volume.

For example, you may want your alarm to ring super loud in the morning, but you want your music to play very low.

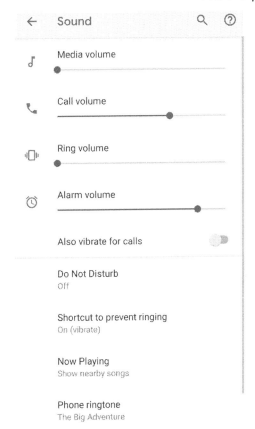

STORAGE

The Pixel has no expandable storage for SD; that means whatever you buy for your phone, that's the amount you have. You can't upgrade it later.

When you first get your phone, storage won't be a big issue, but once you start taking photos (which are larger than you think) and installing apps, it's going to go very quick.

The storage setting helps you manage this. It shows you what's taking up storage, so you can decide if you want to delete things. Just tap on any of the subsections and follow the instructions for what to do to save space.

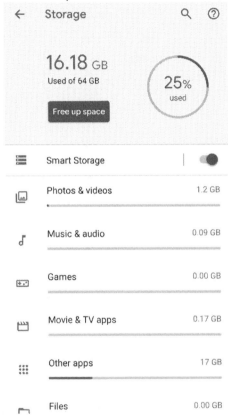

SECURITY & LOCATION

If you want to change your lock screen, add an additional fingerprint, or turn on / off the find your phone setting, you can do it here.

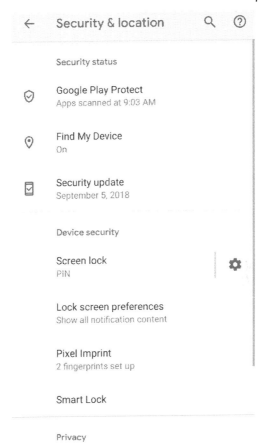

ACCOUNTS

If you have more than one Google account, you can tap on this to add it. If you want to remove your current account, tap on it and tap remove--remember, however, you can have more than one account. Don't remove it just so you can add another.

ACCESSIBILITY

Do you hate phones because the text is too small, the colors are all wrong, you can hear anything? Or something else? That's where accessibility can help. This is where you make changes to the device to make it easier on your eyes or ears.

DIGITAL WELLBEING

Digital wellbeing is my least favorite feature on the Pixel phone; now when my wife says "You spend too much time on your phone"--she can actually prove it! The purpose of the setting is to help you manage your time more. It lets you know your spending 12 hours a day updating your social media with meme's of cats, and "hopefully" make you feel like perhaps you shouldn't do that.

The setting is in beta and isn't perfect. You can see in the example below, for example, that I spent nearly 8 hours in an app called Lollipop. What a time-waster, right? While I technically did spend that much time in the app, what it doesn't show is that Lollipop is a baby monitor and the reason it's so high is that it was on all night.

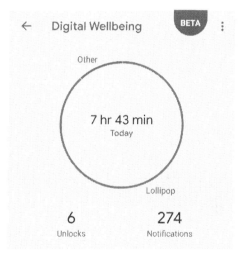

GOOGLE

Google is where you will go to manage any Google device connected with your phone. If you are using a Google watch, for example; or a Chromecast.

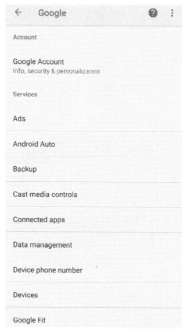

SYSTEM

System is important for one very important reason: system updates. If you don't have your phone set to download updates automatically, then you'll have to do it manually here.

Tap the Advanced button.

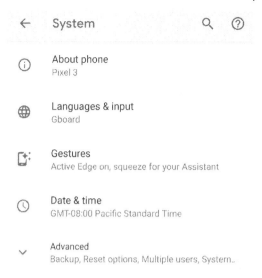

This gives you a menu with more features. One is the System update. If there's an update available, it will say it. If it says it, then tap it.

You'll have to restart your phone before it downloads.

Security update available

This update fixes critical bugs and improves the performance and stability of your Pixel 3. If you download updates over the cellular network or while roaming, additional charges may apply.

Update size: 108.5 MB

Restart now

You can also change the language in this setting as well as make changes to gestures and put limits on users.

TIPS & SUPPORT

This isn't really a setting. It's just tips and support. You can also talk with support here.

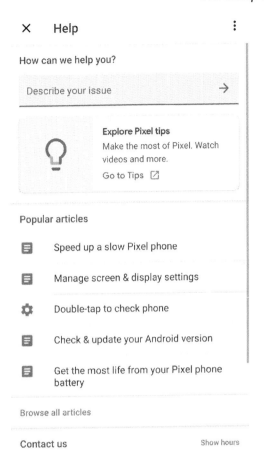

✕   Help   ⋮

How can we help you?

Describe your issue   →

Explore Pixel tips
Make the most of Pixel. Watch videos and more.
Go to Tips ↗

Popular articles

Speed up a slow Pixel phone

Manage screen & display settings

Double-tap to check phone

Check & update your Android version

Get the most life from your Pixel phone battery

Browse all articles

Contact us   Show hours

[7]

ADD-ONS

This chapter will cover:
- Project Fi
- Pixel accessories
- Third-party accessories

PROJECT FI?

In 2015, Google launched something they called Project Fi. It's their vision of what a cell phone network is supposed to be. A shared plan with a healthy amount of data. You pay for what you need--not what the provider tells you. It's sort of a hybrid of using data and using wi-fi to get you good speeds for a price that's quite a bit cheaper than others.

How much cheaper? It depends, but my guess is cheaper than what you are paying.

As of this writing, it starts at $20. That gets you unlimited minutes and text. But no data. Let's say you are a very light data user and only needed 1GB. It would cost you a total of $30--taxes and fees included. If you are a data hog and stream everything you can 24/7, then you would want the top plan 20 GB. That would cost you $80. Total. What if you go over 20GB? Same price! Your speed is slowed--that's the catch. It's guaranteed fast until 20GB, however. According to Google, less than 1% of all people use more than 15GB...so chances are, you'll be fine.

What about families? For a family of six, the most you would pay is $275--that's, again, sharing 20GB. You can see a calculator at https://fi.google.com/about/plan/ .

VR

Google has been pushing VR for quite some time. Is it any good? In my opinion, it's "okay" but it's getting better. The games are not great--they're decent, but not great; there are a few movies; Netflix has VR, but it's basically a movie theater--not the VR you think where you get a 360 view.

The way it works is you slide your phone into a headset, then when you turn your head you get a 360 view. To get to menus, there's a dot and you hover over things by tilting your head to open them.

If you are interested in seeing what VR is all about, then I highly suggest starting with Google Cardboard.

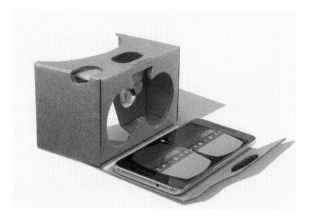

It's $15, and, as the name suggests, made of cardboard; sounds cheap, right? It's surprisingly durable.

If you like it then you can upgrade to the more expensive Daydream View, which is $99 and also includes a remote to make it easier to control.

One of the reasons I also suggest starting with the Cardboard is to see if you get motion sickness. VR makes some people feel dizzy.

PIXEL BUDS

The $159 Pixel Buds is Google's answer to Apple AirPods. Sometimes Google comes out of the gate with something that knocks the socks off the competition. And sometimes it just feels like they whipped something together so they could have something comparable. Personally, the Pixel Buds feel like the latter.

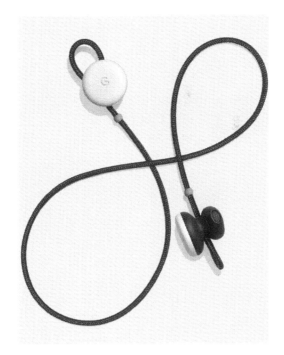

Some people love them. I find that they are harder to keep in your ears then AirPods (which are compatible with Pixel) and just don't feel like the same quality. The strap also gets in the way.

Personal opinions vary, so don't take my word for it.

PIXEL STAND

The $79 Pixel Stand is a stylish way to keep your phone charged. It doubles as a picture frame. If you don't want to plug your phone in and are looking for a good wireless charging solution, then I would start here.

CAMERA LENS

The Pixel has been called the best phone for photographers. Is it? Debatable. But if you are us-

ing it for photos and want to make them even better, then I would consider the $129 Moment lens
and case.

It's a case with a slot to add on a wide angle
lens. Moment sales several different lenses that are
all interchangeable with the case.

There are other lenses out there for much
cheaper, but these lenses typically snap on and are
more flimsy. This gives the photo a less than desir-
able result and it feels more like a gimmicky toy
than a camera lens. The Moment is small but feels
durable and professional. Because of how it at-

taches to the case, there's no change of light leaking in and distorting the image.